First World War
and Army of Occupation
War Diary
France, Belgium and Germany

26 DIVISION
79 Infantry Brigade
Headquarters,
Duke of Cornwall's Light Infantry 8th Battalion,
Devonshire Regiment 10th (Service) Battalion,
Hampshire Regiment 12th (Service) Battalion
and Duke of Edinburgh's (Wiltshire Regiment)
7th Battalion
15 September 1915 - 31 October 1915

WO95/2253/3

The Naval & Military Press Ltd
www.nmarchive.com
Published in association with The National Archives

Published by

The Naval & Military Press Ltd

Unit 10 Ridgewood Industrial Park,
Uckfield, East Sussex,
TN22 5QE England
Tel: +44 (0) 1825 749494

www.naval-military-press.com

www.nmarchive.com

This diary has been reprinted in facsimile from the original. Any imperfections are inevitably reproduced and the quality may fall short of modern type and cartographic standards.

© **Crown Copyright**
Images reproduced by permission of The National Archives, London, England, 2015.

Contents

Document type	Place/Title	Date From	Date To
Heading	WO95/2253/3		
Heading	26th Division 79th Infy Bde Bde Headquarters 10th Bn Devons. Regt 12th Bn Hampshire 7th Bn Wiltshire 8th Bn Duke Of Cornwall's L.I. Sep-Oct 1915		
Heading	26th Division 79th Inf Bde Vol I Sep 15 Oct		
Miscellaneous	War Diary of 79th Infantry Brigade From September 22nd 1915 To September 30th 1915		
War Diary	Sutton Veny	22/09/1915	22/09/1915
War Diary	Boulogne	23/09/1915	23/09/1915
War Diary	Fresnoy-Au-Val	24/09/1915	25/09/1915
War Diary	Pont De Metz	26/09/1915	26/09/1915
War Diary	Cachy	27/09/1915	30/09/1915
Miscellaneous	79th Infantry Brigade Group Order No.1 Appendix II	25/09/1915	25/09/1915
Heading	76th Division 79th Inf. Bde Vol 2 Oct 15		
Heading	79th Infantry Brigade War Diary For October 1915		
War Diary	Cachy	01/10/1915	15/10/1915
War Diary	Villers Bocage	16/10/1915	16/10/1915
War Diary	Cachy	17/10/1915	21/10/1915
War Diary	Villers Bocage	22/10/1915	30/10/1915
War Diary	Sailly Lorette	31/10/1915	31/10/1915
Miscellaneous	79th Infantry Brigade Appendix 1		
Miscellaneous	79th Infantry Brigade Operation Order No. 1 Appendix 15	14/10/1915	14/10/1915
Miscellaneous	79th Brigade Camp	15/10/1915	15/10/1915
Miscellaneous	A Form Messages And Signals		
Miscellaneous	79th Brigade Group Appendix 3	21/10/1915	21/10/1915
Miscellaneous	79th Infantry Brigade Order No. 3		
Heading	26th Division 8th D.C.L.I. Vol I Sep 15 To Oct		
War Diary	Sutton Veny Wilts	15/09/1915	15/09/1915
War Diary	Warminster	22/09/1915	22/09/1915
War Diary	Boulogne	22/09/1915	23/09/1915
War Diary	Seux	24/09/1915	25/09/1915
War Diary	Pont-De-Metz	26/09/1915	26/09/1915
War Diary	Cachy	27/09/1915	30/09/1915
Heading	26th Division 8th D.C.L.I. Vol 2 Oct 15		
War Diary	Cachy-Somme	01/10/1915	09/10/1915
War Diary	Cachy	10/10/1915	14/10/1915
War Diary	Gentelles	15/10/1915	21/10/1915
War Diary	Poulainville	22/10/1915	28/10/1915
War Diary	Albert	29/10/1915	31/10/1915
Heading	26th Division 10th Devonshire Rgt. Vol I Sep 15 To Oct		
War Diary	Sutton Veny	15/09/1915	23/09/1915
War Diary	Boulogne	23/09/1915	26/09/1915
War Diary	Cachy	27/09/1915	30/09/1915
Heading	26th Division 10th Devonshire Regt Vol Oct 15		
War Diary	Cachy	01/10/1915	05/10/1915
War Diary	Cappy	06/10/1915	09/10/1915
War Diary	Cachy	10/10/1915	21/10/1915
War Diary	Coisy	22/10/1915	30/10/1915

War Diary	Sailly Lorette	31/10/1915	31/10/1915
Heading	26th Division 12th Hampshire Regiment Vol I Sep 15 To Oct		
War Diary	Sutton Veny	20/09/1915	20/09/1915
War Diary	Le Havre	21/09/1915	22/09/1915
War Diary	Lonyeau	23/09/1915	23/09/1915
War Diary	Fresnoy-au-val	24/09/1915	25/09/1915
War Diary	Pont-de-Metz	26/09/1915	26/09/1915
War Diary	Gentelles	27/09/1915	30/09/1915
Heading	26th Division 12th Hampshire Vol 2 Oct 15		
War Diary	Gentelles	01/10/1915	07/10/1915
War Diary	Cappy	08/10/1915	11/10/1915
War Diary	Gentelles	12/10/1915	12/10/1915
War Diary	Gentelles	13/10/1915	22/10/1915
War Diary	Cardonette	21/10/1915	29/10/1915
War Diary	Chipilly	30/10/1915	31/10/1915
Heading	26th Division 7th Wiltshires Vol I Sep I 15 To Oct 7		
War Diary	Boulogne	23/09/1915	23/09/1915
War Diary	Courcelles	24/09/1915	24/09/1915
War Diary	Salouel	25/09/1915	25/09/1915
War Diary	Gentelles	26/09/1915	30/09/1915
Heading	26th Division 7th Wiltshires Vol 2 Oct 15		
War Diary	Gentelles	01/10/1915	13/10/1915
War Diary	Villers Bretonneaux	14/10/1915	14/10/1915
War Diary	Villers Bocage	15/10/1915	15/10/1915
War Diary	Villers Bretonneaux	16/10/1915	20/10/1915
War Diary	Villers Bocage	21/10/1915	26/10/1915
War Diary	Frechencourt	27/10/1915	27/10/1915
War Diary	Meaulte	28/10/1915	30/10/1915
War Diary	La Neuville	31/10/1915	31/10/1915

wood (2252) (3)

wood (2252) (3)

26TH DIVISION
79TH INFY BDE

BDE HEADQUARTERS
10TH BN DEVONS. REGT
12TH BN HAMPSHIRE ..
7TH BN WILTSHIRE ..
8TH BN DUKE OF CORNWALL'S L.I.

SEP - OCT 1915

131/6971

76th Division

49th Inf. Bde.
Vol I
Sept. 15 + Oct

Confidential

War Diary

of

79th Infantry Brigade.

from September 22nd, 1915 to September 30th 1915.

79th Infantry Brigade

original

WAR DIARY
INTELLIGENCE SUMMARY
(Erase heading not required.)

Army Form C. 2118.

Place	Date	Hour	Summary of Events and Information	Remarks and references to Appendices
SUTTON VENY	22/9/15	3.20 P.M.	Personnel of Bde H.Q., 8/D.C.L.I., 10/Berks, and 7/Wilts entrained at WARMINSTER and proceeded overseas, their Transport and 12/Hants having moved 2 days previously.	For strength see Appendix i.
BOULOGNE	23/9/15.	10.0 A.M.	The 3 units mentioned above entrained for SALEUX, and marched to a billeting area, where 12/Hants and all transport had preceded them. Bde H.Q. and 12/Hants at FRESNOY-AU-VAL, 10/Berks at PISSY, 8/D.C.L.I. at SEUX, and 7/Wilts at COURCELLES.	Appx.ii. Appx.ii.
FRESNOY-AU-VAL	24/9/15.	4.0 P.M.	G.O.C. III Army inspected 7/Wilts and 12/Hants near COURCELLES.	Appx.ii.
"	25/9/15.	—	The Brigade marched from its billets during the afternoon to fresh billets at PONT DE METZ, except the 7/Wilts, which billeted in SALOUEL. The 116th F.A. Bde, 131st F.Co. R.E., 79th F. Ambulance, and No. 4 Co. Train joined the Brigade from Attd's day, and were billeted in SALEUX.	Appx.ii.
PONT DE METZ	26/9/15	9.30 a.m.	The Brigade marched to fresh billets in CACHY (Hqrs. 10/Berks and 8/D.C.L.I.), GENTELLES (7/Wilts and 12/Hants), and DOMART (remainder of Group and Divisional Cavalry, who joined the Group this day). The infantry were inspected on the march by the XIIIth Army Corps Commander in the morning.	See appendix iii.

WEEKLY STRENGTH.
10/Berks   29. Officers   987. rank and file.
8/D.C.L.I.   30.   "   980.   "   "   "
12/Hants   30.   "   883.   "   "   "
7/Wilts   30.   "   995.   "   "   "

2.

79th Infantry Brigade.

WAR DIARY
of
INTELLIGENCE SUMMARY

Army Form C. 2118.

original

Place	Date	Hour	Summary of Events and Information	Remarks and references to Appendices
CACHY.	27/9/15.		The day was spent in settling into billets; a little company exercise was carried out in each unit.	SgdMM SgdMM
"	28/9/15.		Battalion Drill was carried out in each unit. A course for machine gun officers was started.	
"	29/9/15.		Units were practised in the attack, and did some physical drill.	
"	30/9/15.		Battalion and company work was done. All 4 units were practised in passing through gas in smoke helmets, after being lectured by an expert. Machine gun sections carried out a Brigade Exercise set by the Brigadier.	SgdMM

A.S. Bradbury Brig Genl
C.79.I.B.

Copy No. 15.   War Diary.   Appendix ii.

79th INFANTRY BRIGADE GROUP.

ORDER No. 1

1. The Group will march to-morrow in accordance with the following March Table.

Unit.	Starting Point.	Time.	Route.	To Billet at.
116th F.A.Bde.	Point 65 F'bg de Beauvais AMIENS.	9-15am.	Points 57, 62, St ACHEUL, LONGEAU, and the ROUTE DE ROYE.	DOMART.
131st Co.R.E.	,,	9-45am.	,,	,,
79th Fd.Amb. less 3 Amb. Wagons.	,,	9-47am.	,,	,,
4 Co.Train.	,,	9-50am.	,,	,,
Bde. H.Qrs.	,,	10- 0am.	,,	CACHY.
10th Devons.	,,	10- 0am.	,,	,,
8th D.C.L.I.	,,	10- 5am.	,,	,,
12th Hants.	,,	10-10am.	,,	GENTELLES.
7th Wilts.	,,	10-15am.	,,	,,
3 Amb.Wagons.	,,	10-20am.	As above, and through GENTELLES and CACHY to DOMART.	DOMART.

2. Transport will march in rear of its unit.

3. Infantry Battalions will each send a representative to Brigade H.Qrs at 9 am, when watches will be compared.

4. Billeting parties of Infantry Battalions only will meet the Staff Captain at the starting point at 9am.

5. O.C. 116th F.A.Bde. is arranging the billeting of all other units; the billeting Officers of the 131st F.Co. R.E., F.Ambulance, and Train will report to him to-night for instructions.

6. The Army Corps Commander will inpsect such units as may be passing Point 52 S. of LONGEAU from 12-30pm onwards.

7. The Re-filling Point for the Group to-morrow will be CROSS ROADS E. OF SALEUX West Side of FRENCH barricade. Time of refilling 7am.

7-30pm.
25/9/15.

R.K.Mott
Captain.
Brigade Major 79th Infantry Brigade.

Copies to O.C. each unit.

12/7481

26th review

79th sup. Bat.
vol 2

Oct 15.

Confidential.

79th Infantry Brigade.

War Diary for October, 1915.

79th Infantry Brigade.

Army Form C. 2118.

WAR DIARY
INTELLIGENCE SUMMARY.
(Erase heading not required.)

Instructions regarding War Diaries and Intelligence Summaries are contained in F. S. Regs., Part II. and the Staff Manual respectively. Title pages will be prepared in manuscript.

Place	Date	Hour	Summary of Events and Information	Remarks and references to Appendices
CACHY.	1/10/15	–	The Brigade was employed in Battalion Training, practising attacks from trenches and in the open. Fine.	R.J.M.
"	2/10/15	4.p.m	The Army Commander inspected the 8th D.C.L.I. at VILLERS-BRETONNEUX. Remaining units route-marched and did Battalion drill. Fine.	R.J.M.
"	3/10/15	–	Church parades; 10/Berks' companies route-marched in the afternoon. Drills were carried up. Fine.	R.J.M.
"	4/10/15	–	Units route-marched and did Battalion work. Fine.	R.J.M.
"	5/10/15	–	10/Berks marched to CAPPY, to be attached to the 80th Infy. Brigade for trench-instruction; remaining units drilled or route-marched. A wet day.	R.J.M.
"	6/10/15	–	Nothing to report.	R.J.M.
"	7/10/15	–	Brigadier & Brigade Major visited 3 Bde H.Qrs. at the front, and the trenches occupied by the 4/K.R.R., to whom 10/Berks were attached, near FRISE.	R.J.M.
"	8/10/15	–	14/Hants marched to CAPPY, & be attached to the 80th Infy. Bde for trench-instruction.	R.J.M.
"	9/10/15	–	Nothing to report, except that the 10/Berks returned to CACHY; they had no casualties whilst in the trenches.	R.J.M.
"	10/10/15	–	8/D.C.L.I. marched out to be attached to the 81st Infy Bde for trench-instruction, but were recalled before they had gone beyond LAMOTTE-EN-SANTERRE, owing to change of plans.	R.J.M.
"	11/10/15	–	10/Hants reported a man drowned during a bathing-parade.	R.J.M.
"	12/10/15	–	14/Hants returned from the trenches; they had no casualties, except the man drowned.	R.J.M.
"	13/10/15	–	Colonel Pyke-Walker handed over command of the 12/Hants to Lt.Colonel B. Majendie, K.R.R., the former returning to England.	R.J.M.
"	14/10/15	–	7/K.R.R. moved from GENTELLES to VILLERS-BRETONNEUX, and 8/D.C.L.I. from CACHY to GENTELLES.	R.J.M.

79th Infantry Brigade.

WAR DIARY
INTELLIGENCE SUMMARY.

Army Form C. 2118.

Place	Date	Hour	Summary of Events and Information	Remarks and references to Appendices
15.10.15. CACHY.	15/10/15.	6.15.a.m.	The Brigade marched out to take part in a Tactical exercise. Think fog for some time after starting; halted between CORBIE and PONT NOYELLES the Army Commander watched the Brigade march by him. Tactical situation was given on arrival at PONT NOYELLES, and eventually the Brigade got into a position of deployment N. of QUERRIEUX. After the men's dinners the Brigade Staff went on to S^t. GRATIEN, and took part in a further Tactical scheme, whilst the Brigade marched to VILLERS BOCAGE, arriving there at 6.30 p.m. and billeted there. Headquarters billeting in MONTONVILLERS.	Appendix 1. R.J.R.M.
VILLERS BOCAGE	16/10/15.	7.15.a.m.	Marched back to Old billets. the Army Corps Commander watching the Brigade as it passed through CORBIE. These 2 days' marching was a big trial, and in testimony came through very creditably, only 7 men having to be picked up by the ambulance. Nothing worthy of report.	Appendix 2. R.J.R.M. R.J.R.M.
CACHY	17 to 20/10/15.	—		
"	21/10/15.	9.30.a.m.	The Brigade moved into fresh billets in the area of VILLERS-BOCAGE, where they were distributed as follows:-	Appendix 3. R.J.R.M.

VILLERS BOCAGE Bde H.Q.
Stadtmars of Div: General School.
7/W.R.
1311 F.Co. R.E.
79th F. Ambulance.

COISY — 10/Kenson.
4 Coy. Train.
POULAINVILLE — 8/B.C.L.I.
CARDONNETTE — 12/Hants.

Foggy early; then warm and fine. Brigade marched well, very few men falling out.

3.

79th Infantry Brigade

Army Form C. 2118.

WAR DIARY
or
INTELLIGENCE SUMMARY.

(Erase heading not required.)

Place	Date	Hour	Summary of Events and Information	Remarks and references to Appendices
VILLERS BOCAGE	24/10/15 – 26/10/15		Nothing to report.	AJP
VILLERS BOCAGE	27/10/15	—	7/N.F. moved from VILLERS-BOCAGE to FRECHENCOURT. 8/D.C.L.I. moved from POULAINVILLE to ST GRATIEN.	AJP
"	28/10/15	—	7/N.F. moved from FRECHENCOURT to MEAULTE, to be attached to 54th Bde for trench instruction. 8/D.C.L.I. moved from ST GRATIEN to ALBERT, to be attached to 5th Bde for trench instruction.	AJP
"	29/10/15	—	2 Companies 12/Hants moved from CARDONETTE to VAUX-SUR-SOMME. Bde HQ, and remainder of 12/Hants moved from VILLERS BOCAGE, COISY, and CARDONETTE, to 2 former units to SAILLY LORETTE, and the latter to CHIPILLY.	Appendix 4 AJP
"	30/10/15	9 a.m.	2 Companies 12/Hants moved from VAUX-SUR-SOMME to ETINEHEM. It had been the intention to attach the Brigade to the 5th Division for trench instruction, but orders were received cancelling the previous arrangements. 1 Company 12/Hants were moved from ETINEHEM to CHIPILLY.	AJP
SAILLY LORETTE	31/10/15	—	It is suggested that in training the New Armies in England attention should be paid to the training of Brigade Tunnelling Companies. These Companies are at present found from men trained in Infantry Battalions not seem a waste of train & to do so, if they are to be used as Tunnellers when they are sent to France.	

31/10/15

A.J. Poole Brig Genl
79 Inf Bde

Appendix 1.

79th INFANTRY BRIGADE.

STRENGTH on marching out from SUTTON VENY.

@@@@@@@@@@@@@@

BRIGADE HEADQUARTERS.

Brigadier General A. J. Poole.

Captain R.J.K.Mott.   Brigade Major.

Captain L.J.Castle.   Staff Captain.

Lieut: H.G.Wimbush.   Brigade M/c Gun Officer.

Lieut: R.E.Threlfall. R.E.   Bgde. Signalling Officer.

Other ranks as per War Establishment.

@@@@@@@@

Unit.	Officers.	Other ranks. including attached.	Totals.
10th Devons.	30	957	987
8th D.C.L.Infy.	30	988	1,018
12th Hants.	30	893	923
7th Wilts.	30	995	1,025
	120.	3,833	3,953

Appendix 1.

79th INFANTRY BRIGADE.

Copy No. 15

OPERATION ORDER No. 1.*

1. The Brigade will march from its present billets to-morrow.

2. MARCH TABLE

Order of March.	Starting Point.	Time.	Route.	Remarks.
Brigade H.Q.	N.end of CACHY.	6-15am.	FOUILLOY - CORBIE - PONT NOYELLES.	
10th Devons.	,,	6-15am.	,,	
12th Hants.	Cross roads N.N.W. of GENTELLES.	6-0am.	,,	
8th D.C.L.I.	,,	6-5am.	,,	
7th Wilts.	Cross roads near Pt.40, 1 mile N.W.of VILLERS-BRETONNEUX.	7-20am.	,,	
Brigaded M/c Guns & their S.A.A.Carts.	As for their Units.	------	,,	Machine Guns & Transport march in rear of Units until joining the Column, and then take their places as shewn in the Order of March.
Brigaded First Line Transport.	As for their Units.	------	,,	
No. 4 Coy: Train.	N.end of CACHY.	6-30am.	,,	
Section 79th Fd.Ambulance.	,,	6-35am.	,,	

3. Baggage Wagons, containing blankets, will accompany the Column.

4. Supply Wagons will refill at the usual refilling point, in time to take their places as the Column passes that point.

H.Q.79th Bde.   (Sgd) R. J. K. Mott. Captain.

14/10/15.   Brigade Major 79th Infantry Brigade.

No. 1 Copy to Devons.
    2. ,, D.C.L.I
    3. ,, Hants.
    4. ,, Wilts.
    5. ,, Bde.Transport Officer.
    6. ,, O.C.No.4 Coy: Train.
    7. ,, Bde. Supply Officer.
    8. ,, O.C.79th Fd.Amb.
    9. ,, O i/c Section Fd.Amb.
  10. ,, Division.
  11. ,, G. O. C.
  12. ,, Bde. Major.
  13. ,, Staff Captain.
  14. ,, Bde. M.G.O.
  15. ,, War Diary.
  16. ,, Files.

* should have been numbered 2.

Appendix 2.
Copy No 8.

79th Brigade Group

1. The B'de Group will return to its billets in the B'de area tomorrow.

2.   MARCH TABLE.

Order of March	Starting Pt	Time	Route
B'de H.Q.		7.15 am	
7/Wilts	"V"	7.15	RAINNEVILLE –
8/2 C.L.I.	of	7.20	QUERRIEUX –
14/Hants	VILLERS	7.25	PONT NOYELLES
14/Devons	BOCAGE	7.30	– CORBIE –
Balance of 1st Line T'prt		7.35	FOUILLOY
2nd Line T'pt		7.40	
79th F. Amb:		7.45	

3. Order of March of 1st Line Transport is shown on attached.

Issued at 6. p.m.
15.10.15.

R.J.K. Mitt Capt
B.M. 79 I. Bde

"A" Form.
MESSAGES AND SIGNALS.
Army Form C. 2121.

TO	Office Copy

Copy No 1 to	Wilts	✓
	2 -	DCLI	✓
	3 -	Hants	✓
	4 -	Devons	✓
	5 -	Bde Tpt Officer	✓
	6 -	4 Coy Train	✓
	7 -	79 F. Amb.	✓
	8 -	Office Copy	✓
	9 -	Staff Captain	✓
	10 -	Bde Major	✓

Appendix 3. War Diary.

~ 79th BRIGADE GROUP. ~

1. The Brigade Group, less Artillery, will march ~~tomorrow~~ today as under:

Unit.	Starting Point.	Time.	Route.	Remarks.
Bde: Hd:Qrs. Grenade School H.Q. & Details	E. end of CACHY	9.30.a.m.	CORBIE — PONT NOYELLES.	
12/Hants.	"	9.30. "	"	
9/DCLI.	"	9.35. "	"	
10/Devons.	"	9.40. "	"	
7/Wilts.	Pt. 40, one mile N.W. of VILLERS-BRETONNEUX	10.35. "	"	
131st Fd: Co: R.E.	E. end of CACHY	9.45. "	"	
X 1st Line Transport.	"	9.50. "	"	X except that of 7/Wilts, which will join the column at their starting-point.
No.4.Coy: Train.	"	9.55. "	"	
79th Fd: Amb:	"	10.0. "	"	

2. Blanket wagons will report at Headquarters of Units at 8am tomorrow; should they not be ready to move off at the same time as units, parties must be left to load and accompany the wagons. In this case O.C. Units must report the situation to Bde: Hd: Qrs: as soon as possible after moving off.

3. Baggage Wagons (and Blanket Wagons ~~if ready~~) will join the Train Coy. at CACHY, except those of 7/Wilts, which will join at their starting-point.

4. Instructions regarding re-filling ~~tomorrow~~ today will be issued later.

Issued at 9.a.m.
21/10/15.

R.J.K. Mott.
Captain
Bde: Major 79th Brigade Group.

S E C R E T. Copy No. 8.

79th INFANTRY BRIGADE order No. 3.

28th October 1915.

With reference to 5th Divisional Order No.75 (a copy of which has been forwarded to all concerned) the moves of Brigade Headqrs.; 10th Devons and 12th Hants will take place in accordance with the following March Table.

Units.	Starting Point.	Time.	Destination.	Route.	Remarks.
				29th OCTOBER.	
12th Hants. (2 Coys)	CARDONETTE.	---	VAUX-SUR-SOMME	ALLONVILLE - QUERRIEUX - PONTNOYELLES - CORBIE.	Arrival to be reported to 15th Inf.Bde. at SAILLY LORETTE. Billeting party to report at Noon to Adjutant, 11th Scottish Rifles, at VAUX.
				30th OCTOBER.	
Bde. H. Qrs.	VILLERS-BOCAGE.	9-0am.	SAILLY LORETTE	Do.	Billeting arrangements in accordance with 5th Div: Order No.75 dated 27th Octr. Billeting parties report to Staff Captain 79th Infantry Brigade at SAILLY LORETTE at 10 - 0am.
12th Hants. (less 2 Coys)	Cross roads ½ mile N.W. of ALLONVILLE.	9-0am.	CHIPILLY.	Do.	
10th Devons.	Do.	---	SAILLY LORETTE	Do.	
12th Hants. (2 Coys)	VAUX-SUR-SOMME	9-5am.	ETINEHEM.	---	Billeting party to report to DAQMG. 5th Div: H.Qrs. at ETINEHEM at 11 am.

Issued at 10-30am.

Copies to 10th Devons.
12th Hants.
2 6th Division.
4 Co. Train.
G. O. C.
Brigade Major.
Staff Captain.
War Diary
File.

Captain.

Brigade Major 79th Infantry Brigade.

Appendix 4.

79/36 Kuwain

St Seals.
Vol I
Sept. 15 + Oct

Army Form C. 2118.

WAR DIARY
or
INTELLIGENCE SUMMARY.

8th (Service) Batt.
Duke of Cornwalls Light Infantry.
B.E.F.

(Erase heading not required.)

Place	Date 1915	Hour	Summary of Events and Information	Remarks and references to Appendices
Sutton Veny, Wilts.	15 Sep		Battalion received orders to embark for service with British Expeditionary Force.	
Warminster	22 "	3/a.m.	Battalion left Warminster and embarked for France via Folkestone and Boulogne.	
Boulogne	22 "	11-30 p.m	Arrived at Boulogne and proceeded to Rest Camp.	
do.	23 "	10 p.m	Entrained for Saleux and marched that evening in pouring rain to Billets at Seux - Somme.	
Seux.	24 "	—	In Billets at Seux.	
	25 "	12-30 p.m	Marched to Pont-de-Metz. Arrived in darkness, billeted there. Bad billets	
Pont-de-Metz	26 "	10 a.m.	Marched to Cachy via Amiens - Long march, raining, good billets.	
Cachy	27 "	—	remained at Cachy - first pay day - wet - good war news.	
do	28 "	—	remained at Cachy - Battalion Exercise.	
do	29 "	—	remained at Cachy - do.	
do	30 "	—	remained at Cachy - do. and experimenting with Gas Helmets.	

Cachy.
30 Sep 1915

J.H. Wereclyde, Colonel.
Commdg. 8E(S)Bn. D. of Corn. L.I.

12/7608

H H Kurein

8th sed.
vol 2

Oct. 15

2

Report No II.

CONFIDENTIAL.

Army Form C. 2118.

WAR DIARY

of

8th (Service) Batn.

INTELLIGENCE SUMMARY. Duke of Cornwall's Light Infantry.
B.E.F.

(Erase heading not required.)

Instructions regarding War Diaries and Intelligence Summaries are contained in F. S. Regs., Part II. and the Staff Manual respectively. Title pages will be prepared in manuscript.

Place	Date 1915	Hour	Summary of Events and Information	Remarks and references to Appendices
CACHY-SOMME	1 Oct to 9th Oct		Remained at CACHY, Battalion employed in Battalion & Company Exercises, Route Marching & Digging	
CACHY-	10th Oct.	10:50 a.m.	Battalion left CACHY for attachment to 81st Inf. Brigade for instruction in Trench Warfare — on arrival at LAMOTTE order to proceed cancelled. Went 2nd Battalion at LAMOTTE — returned to Billets.	
CACHY-	11th to 13th		Remained at CACHY.	
CACHY.	14th Oct	3 pm.	Moved to GENTELLES — one mile distant — Good Billets.	
GENTELLES	15th —	6 a.m.	Brigade exercise — Billeted at VILLERS BOCAGE. 20 miles distant.	
—	16th —		do. — returned to Billets.	
GENTELLES	17th to 20th		Remained at GENTELLES — Commenced repairing Billets.	
do.	21st —	9 a.m.	Left GENTELLES and marched to POULAINVILLE. 18 miles.	
POULAINVILLE.	22nd to 26th		Remained at POULAINVILLE.	
do	27th —		Marched to ST GRATIEN.	
—	28th —		Marched to ALBERT. Billeted there.	
ALBERT.	29th —		"A" + "B" Coys. in trenches — attached for instruction to 6th Berkshire Regt and 8th Suffolks respectively. "C" + "D" Coys employed on defences of ALBERT.	
do.	30th =		"A" + "B" Coys still in trenches, first casualty, "C" Coy "B" Coy killed by Rifle Grenade. "C" + "D" Coy working on defences.	
do.	31st =		Sudden order received to move, Companies recalled from trenches and works, (town continuously shelled), Whole Battalion marched to LA NEUVILLE in evening.	

LA NEUVILLE,
31 Oct. 1915.

J. W. Vera Cloyd Colonel
Commanding 8th (S) Bn. D. of Corn. L.I.

12/6930

26/79

36th Division

10th Devonshire Regt.
Vol I

Sept. 15 + 001

Less Mag 19

WAR DIARY or INTELLIGENCE SUMMARY

Army Form C. 2118.

(Erase heading not required.)

Instructions regarding War Diaries and Intelligence Summaries are contained in F. S. Regs., Part II. and the Staff Manual respectively. Title pages will be prepared in manuscript.

ORDERLY ROOM RECD 30 SEP.1915
10th (SERVICE) BN. DEVON R.

Place	Date	Hour	Summary of Events and Information	Remarks and references to Appendices
Sutton Veny	15/9/15	—	Orders recd to embark for overseas on 21/9/15	(see)
— " —	20/9/15	4.45am	All Regtl. Transport & 108 N.C.O.s & men., Maj. Hens, Lt. Dunning & 2/Lt. Taylor — Left Warminster Stn. by 6.20 am. Train for Southampton & Havre.	(see)
— " —	22/9/15 23/9/15	4 pm	Returned at Warminster. (2 Trains) Arrive Folkestone & Crossed to Boulogne — arr 2.115am. 834 Rank & File. Went into Rest Camp at Ostrohove. (26 Officers)	(see)
Boulogne	23/9/15	12.30pm	Battn entrained at Gare Centrale. Arrived at SALEUX 5.35 pm. marched to PISSY (in thunderstorm). Quartered in Billets. the Transport & advanced party already in Billets at PISSY.	(see)
— " —	25/9/15 26/9/15	2 p.m.	Marched to Billets at PONT-DE-METZ (AMIENS). Whole Brigade here. Very wet. Marched to Billets at CACHY (11 miles) Dull weather good for marching.	(see)
CACHY	27 28 Sept 29 30		Remained in Billets at CACHY & continued training. 30 Officers. 950 Rank & File. Strength of Battn.	(see)

F.W. Williams
Comdg Col. 10th Devon Regt.

121/74 S/

26/74

26th K. Hussein

To Bemohin Regr.
10-Bemohin
vol 2

Oct 15.

Army Form C. 2118.

WAR DIARY
INTELLIGENCE SUMMARY.
(Erase heading not required.)

Instructions regarding War Diaries and Intelligence Summaries are contained in F. S. Regs., Part II. and the Staff Manual respectively. Title pages will be prepared in manuscript.

ORDERLY ROOM
REC'D
31 OCT. 1915
No.
10TH (SERVICE) BN. DEVON REGT.

Place	Date	Hour	Summary of Events and Information	Remarks and references to Appendices
CACHY	1915 Oct. 1st		Continued training. Heavy firing heard to NE during day & evening. Saw aeroplanes being shelled S.E. & N.E. nationality of aeroplanes could not be distinguished. Gas-helmets tested in Gas Chamber.	
" "	2 Oct.		}	
" "	3 "		} Continued Training in Billets. Nothing to report	
" "	4 "		}	
" "	5 "	9 p.m.	Battⁿ. (less machine gun section) marched to CAPPY via MERRICOURT arrived 4 a.m. & went into Billets for the night. Weather cold and wet. Roads very muddy. No men fell out. (March about 17 miles)	
CAPPY	6 Oct		O.C. Coys. Adjt. & 2 Sergts per Coy visited trenches 9.30 a.m.	
" "	6 Oct	6 p.m.	"A" & "B" Coys attached to 4th Rifle Bde. ——— Hd. Qrs. & "C" & "D" Coys attached to 4th K.R.R. marched into trenches for instruction	
" "	7 Oct		Remained in trenches for instruction	
" "	8 Oct	5.15 p.m.	All Coys. left trenches & returned to CAPPY for the night. During stay in trenches here were no casualties. Nothing of importance. 6th & 7th surfing by day & night. Some rifle grenades & french mortar fire. Shells also a few. No damage done.	
CAPPY	9 Oct	4.30 a.m.	Baggage left for CACHY. Battⁿ marched off at 5.30 a.m. no men fell out. Marched via CACHY 12 noon.	

WAR DIARY or INTELLIGENCE SUMMARY

Army Form C. 2118.

Place	Date	Hour	Summary of Events and Information	Remarks and references to Appendices
CACHY	1915 10th Oct		Continued training in Billets. Heavy gunfire heard to N.E. during afternoon.	Copy
"	11th			
"	12th		11th to 13th. Lieut. A.W. Peck appointed Asst Instructor at School of Instruction for	Copy
"	13th		Bathing &c report.	
"	14th			
	15th	6.15 am	Brigade took part in a "Tactical Exercise" under Corps Commander. Marched via CORBIE – QUERRIEUX – BOCAGE (arrived at 7 p.m.) Marched about 17 miles.	Copy
	16th	7.0 am	VILLERS-BOCAGE (arrived at 7 pm) Marched back to Billets at CACHY, arrived 2 pm. (Battn. under Bde Maj / Scott)	Copy
CACHY	17th		Continued training in Billets	
"	18th			Copy
"	19th			
"	20th	2.30 pm	Recd. orders to be ready to move tomorrow. Destination unknown.	
"	21st	9 am	Bn. marched via CORBIE – QUERRIEUX & COISY & villages near by. Bde. HQ.	Copy
COISY	22nd		at VILLERS-BOCAGE. Arrived 5/1 m. Dense mist most of day. Continued training in Billets.	Copy
"	23rd	1.35 pm	Enemy Biplane (apparently a "RUMPLER") passed over village very high pursued by one of our aeroplanes. Direction of flight 230° (G. mag)	Copy

NOTE Lieut & Mr T.N. Carlis proceed to England to take up duties of Works Officer at Warwick

Army Form C. 2118.

WAR DIARY
or
INTELLIGENCE SUMMARY.
(Erase heading not required.)

Place	Date	Hour	Summary of Events and Information	Remarks and references to Appendices
COISY	1915 24th Oct		Continued training in Billets	
"	25"		" " " "	
"	26"		" " French observation balloon, apparently broken adrift, passed over the village about 12 noon in N.W. direction. Acceptance in attendance.	
"	27"		Signalling communication with balloon. Very heavy firing audible from NE nearly all day. Wind strong NE.	
"	28"		Continued training in Billets. Nothing to report	
"	29"			
"			Recd orders for Brigade to be attached to 5th Divn for training in French work. Sn Bn to be attached to a 1st Inf Bde from 31st. Proceed to trenches tomorrow + one to SUZANNE on 30th. hour 12, 2 Coys to trenches till 3rd hour. hour 3rd, 2 Coys to Trenches till 5th hour.	
	30"		Marched to SAILLY-LAURETTE & sent out Billets	
SAILLY LORETTE	31"		Been move to SUZANNE cancelled. Awaiting instructions	

G. Sherwood Col.
Comdg 10th Bn. Devon Regt.

79/26

121/6991

36th Brown

12th Hampshire Regiment.

vol I

Sept. 15 + Oct

Army Form C. 2118.

WAR DIARY
or
INTELLIGENCE SUMMARY.
(Erase heading not required.)

12th (S) B'n — The Hampshire Regt

Instructions regarding War Diaries and Intelligence Summaries are contained in F.S. Regs., Part II. and the Staff Manual respectively. Title pages will be prepared in manuscript.

Place	Date	Hour	Summary of Events and Information	Remarks and references to Appendices
Witton Ferry	20/9/15	9 a.m.	Left by train, arrived Southampton 11 a.m. Embarked. Sailed 5 p.m. for Havre. Weather fine.	
Le Havre	21/9/15	7 a.m.	Disembarked. Marched Rest Camp. Weather fine. Passage normal.	
Havre	22/9/15	9 a.m.	Marched to Station. Entrained. Training all day. Arrived Lingnan 11.15 p.m. Detrained. Weather hot.	
Lingnan	23/9/15	11.15 p.m.	Started march to Iversny-au-Val. Bivouacked en route. Arrived 3 p.m. Billeted. Weather hot & wet.	
Iversny-au-Val	24/9/15	6 p.m.	Marched up in morning. Inspected by A.O.C. 9th Army at 6 in afternoon. Movement at 4 p.m. Weather raining.	
Iversny-au-Val	25/9/15	9 a.m.	Left at 11.30 am. Marched to Pont-de-Metz, arrived 5.30 pm. Billeted. Weather very wet.	
Pont-de-Metz	26/9/15	9 a.m.	Left at 9.30. Marched to Fontelles. arrived at 3.15. Billeted en route by A.O.C. 12th Army Corps. Weather dull. Billets.	
Fontelles	27/9/15	6 hr	Cleaned at Parade &c. Weather showery.	
Fontelles	28/9/15	6 hr	Coy's. Baths. Present strike rate marches. Weather cloudy, cold.	
Fontelles	29/9/15	6 hr	Coy's Work. Present still. Bayonet Exercise. route marches within scenery. Weather dull. Showery.	
Fontelles	30/9/15	6 hr	Coy's work in morning. Lectures & Officers & N.C. Officers afternoon &c. Lecture on Gas. Helmets and practical experience of gas. Weather fine, cold.	

121/7608

John Kværn

12k Hauptsthei
vol: 2

Oct 15

G.2
3 sheet

Army Form C. 2118.

WAR DIARY
or
INTELLIGENCE SUMMARY.

(Erase heading not required.)

12 -/19 02- The Hampshire Regt

Instructions regarding War Diaries and Intelligence Summaries are contained in F. S. Regs., Part II. and the Staff Manual respectively. Title pages will be prepared in manuscript.

Place	Date	Hour	Summary of Events and Information	Remarks and references to Appendices
Gontelles	1/10/15	6 p.m.	Practice in the march from trenches in evening. Afternoon Company Parades. Showery, gone cold.	
Gontelles	2/10/15	6 p.m.	Company Parades all day as on morning. Afternoon Battalion practised in assault. Fine, chilly, warmer	
Gontelles	3/10/15	6 p.m.	Church Parade (Sunday) 10 am. Platoon Company. Afternoon. Weather finer, dull	
Gontelles	4/10/15	6 p.m.	Regt. moved from camp. Platoon Company. Afternoon platoon assault, bayonet fighting. Weather cold	
Gontelles	5/10/15	6 p.m.	Reg paraded 9-11 am. Brigade night attack commenced at 10 pm until afternoon. Very wet & rainy. Heavy rain.	
Gontelles	6/10/15	6 p.m.	Regt. returned 4 am. Platoon and afternoon Company work. Afternoon fire	
Gontelles	7/10/15	6 p.m.	Battn. Attd training. Morning, afternoon Company work. Glow & rainy. Weather fine	
Guy	8/10/15	6 p.m.	Left at 2.25 for Guy, arrived 3th. 4.30 pm. April march. Weather dull but fine	
Guy	9/10/15	6 p.m.	Bullet of Beth to Billets occupied, 11 officers. 59 men in morning. Afternoon platoon drill. Pt. Wait	
Cuffy	10/10/15	6 p.m.	Instructed ½ C & D Companies in Trench work. 32nd H.R.R.I. 92 relieved platoons of tubes 2nd Hi April, tomorrow 2.30 p.m. Weather dull	
Cuffy	11/10/15	6 p.m.	In trenches. Weather fine & warm.	
Gontelles	12/10/15	6 p.m.	2 Trenches. Fine morning, wet afternoon. Regt left Trenches at 6.30 am arrived Guy 7.30. Weather fine, dry. Cloudy 8 pm.	
Gontelles	13/10/15	6 p.m.	Morning Pl & platoon, Rifle inspection. Wet afternoon and Inter-Company afternoon. Cloudy. C.O. Lt Walker left the Battalion & took command of Brigade. 4th R.M.R. took over the Command. Weather dull to fine warm	
Gontelles	14/10/15	6 p.m.	Reg. and afternoon Company work. 4.E.C. Chapandi inspected Battalion at 5 day also Transport, found the command	
Willers Bocage	15/10/15	8 p.m.	12th Army Corps. G.O.C. Brigadier General, all inspected Battalion much in many Weather still warm	
Gontelles	16/10/15	6 p.m.	Left Gontelles 6 am marched to Willers Bocage about 20 miles. Finished excursion for Raglan. Pl. 2nd H Brigade made this day	
Gontelles	17/10/15	6 p.m.	Reg. at Army Corps Command. Ordnes. Weather calm, still, wet, 3 & 6 pm warm.	
Gontelles	18/10/15	6 p.m.	Left Willers Bocage 7.30 am Brigade Route March, arrived Gontelles 3 pm. Brighter calm, much to fine, warm	
Gontelles	19/10/15	6 p.m.	Ottawa D. antlers Sunday. Church Parade 10.30 am. Weather calm fine warm	
Gontelles	20/10/15	6 p.m.	Route March Pts 10 am. afternoon, fine, warm by Lieut Ballard & Captains. Weather fine much weather	
Gontelles	21/10/15	6 p.m.	Route march morn, afternoon Company work. Weather dull, warm calm	
Gontelles	22/10/15	6 p.m.	Company Parade, drill. Fine warm calm	
Gontelles	23/10/15	6 p.m.	Left Gontelles 9.20 am against Callette & 45 Dublin. Weather fine warm calm	
	24/10/15	6 p.m.	Church Parade. Divine Service. Weather fine warm calm	

Army Form C. 2118.

WAR DIARY
or
INTELLIGENCE SUMMARY.
(Erase heading not required.)

Instructions regarding War Diaries and Intelligence Summaries are contained in F. S. Regs., Part II. and the Staff Manual respectively. Title pages will be prepared in manuscript.

Place	Date	Hour	Summary of Events and Information	Remarks and references to Appendices
Cardonette	23/10/15	6p	Company work. Weather fine, warm, calm.	
Cardonette	24/10/15	6p	Sunday. Church Parade 10 a.m. Weather dull and cold, rain at night.	
Cardonette	25/10/15	6p	Battalion drill and Company work. Weather showery and cold.	
Cardonette	26/10/15	6p	Battalion work and Company work. Weather fine, humid, cold.	
Cardonette	27/10/15	6p	Battalion Route March. Weather calm, rainy, cold.	
Cardonette	28/10/15	6p	Company work. Bivouac & economy. Weather cold and cold.	
Cardonette	29/10/15	6p	C. and D. Companies left at 9.30 a.m. to be billeted at Vaux and to proceed next day to billets at Etinehem, under Major Wadsworth. Company work for A & B. Companies. Weather dull, warmer, calm.	
Chipilly	30/10/15	6p	A & B Companies left Cardonette 9 a.m. marched to Chipilly arriving 3.30 p. billeted. C & D Companies left Vaux-sur-Somme 10.15 marched to Etinehem billeted. Weather calm dull.	
Chipilly	31/10/15	6p	Sunday. Voluntary Church Parade for A & B. Co. Orders to Etinehem received. C & D. Co. left Etinehem & marched to Chipilly, to billets. Weather calm, dull, damp, cold.	

12/
7083

36th Division

7th Wiltshire
Vol I

Sept 15 + Oct

Army Form C. 2118.

WAR DIARY
or
INTELLIGENCE SUMMARY. 1/1A

(Erase heading not required.)

Instructions regarding War Diaries and Intelligence Summaries are contained in F. S. Regs., Part II. and the Staff Manual respectively. Title pages will be prepared in manuscript.

Place	Date	Hour	Summary of Events and Information	Remarks and references to Appendices
BOULOGNE	23/9/15	10 am	On September 22nd 1915 the 7th (S) Battalion East Wilts Regiment marched out of SUTTON VENY at 3 pms and entrained for FOLKESTONE. FOLKESTONE was reached at 10.30 pm and the regiment at once embarked for BOULOGNE which was reached at 1.30 am 23.9.15. The crossing was calm. On disembarking the regiment marched up about 3 miles to a rest Camp above BOULOGNE reached at about 2.30 am 23.9.15. Parade was ordered at 1 pm, and the Battalion marched to the Central Station BOULOGNE and entrained for SALEUX arriving at 8.15 pm. From SALEUX we marched to COURCELLES and billeted for the night reaching our billets about 12 pm. The weather during this day was very hot and during the march to COURCELLES very heavy rain was experienced. Strength 30 officers 1014 other Ranks	1/1A
COURCELLES	24/9/15	11 am	On 24.9.15 the regiment remained in COURCELLES and was inspected by General Munro Commander of the III army at 4 pm who expressed the greatest satisfaction with the regiment. It rained during the whole day. Strength 30 officers 1015 other ranks	1/1A
SALOUEL	25/9/15	9 am	The next day the regiment paraded at 1 pm and marched with the 79 Brigade to SALOUEL where it billeted for the night. The weather was again bad the march was about 11 miles	1/1A

Army Form C. 2118.

WAR DIARY
or
INTELLIGENCE SUMMARY.

(Erase heading not required.)

Place	Date	Hour	Summary of Events and Information	Remarks and references to Appendices
GENTELLES	26/9/15	6pm	On the morning of 26th parade was ordered at 9.30 am and the Battalion marched to Billets at GENTELLES covering about 3 pm. Distance about 12 miles. A halt was made for dinner during the march. On the line of march the Brigade was inspected by General Wilson the Corps Commander. Weather dull and showery. Strength 30 Officers 1009 other ranks. 5 NCOs to Hospital	
GENTELLES	27/9/15	10 am	Remained in Billets at GENTELLES. Weather dull & showery. Strength 30 Officers 1011 other ranks two returning from Hospital	
GENTELLES	28/9/15	10 am	Remained in Billets at GENTELLES. Weather dull & showery. Strength 30 Officers 1005 other ranks 6 ASC men attached returned to their Unit eg ASC 28th Div Train.	
GENTELLES	29/9/15	10 am	Remained in Billets at GENTELLES. Weather dull & showery. Strength 30 Officers 1006 other ranks 1 n CO returned from Hospital	
GENTELLES	30/9/15	6 pm	Remained in Billets at GENTELLES. Weather fine & cold. Strength 30 Officers 1008 other ranks inclusive of attached	

A.J. Stanchill Capt Act for OC
9th (S) Batt Worc Regt

12/7431

26th Brown

yr Wiltshire
vol 2.

Oct 15

Army Form C. 2118.

WAR DIARY
or
INTELLIGENCE SUMMARY.

(Erase heading not required.)

Place	Date	Hour	Summary of Events and Information	Remarks and references to Appendices
GENTELLES	1/10/15	6pm	Remained in billets at GENTELLES weather fine & cold Strength 30 officers 1006 other ranks in chevaux yattacked	Lyf
GENTELLES	2/10/15	6pm	Remained in billets at GENTELLES weather fine & cold Strength 30 officers 1006 other ranks in chevaux yattached.	Lyf
GENTELLES	3/10/15	6pm	Remained in billets at GENTELLES weather fine & frosty Strength 30 officers 1006 other ranks in chevaux yattached	Lyf
GENTELLES	4/10/15	6pm	Remained in billets at GENTELLES weather showery Strength 30 officers 1006 other ranks in chevaux yattacked	Lyf
GENTELLES	5/10/15	6pm	Returned to billets at GENTELLES weather showery Strength 30 officers 1005 other ranks in chevaux yattached 1 RAMC Lcpl returned to H.Qs Division.	Lyf
GENTELLES	6/10/15	6pm	Remained in billets at GENTELLES weather fine & cold Strength 30 officers 1005 other ranks	Lyf
GENTELLES	7/10/15	6pm	Remained in billets at GENTELLES weather fine & cold Strength 30 officers 1005 other ranks	Lyf
GENTELLES	8/10/15	6pm	Remained in billets at GENTELLES weather fine & cold Strength 30 officers 1005 other ranks	Lyf

Army Form C. 2118.

WAR DIARY
or
INTELLIGENCE SUMMARY.

(Erase heading not required.)

Place	Date	Hour	Summary of Events and Information	Remarks and references to Appendices
GENTELLES	9/10/15	6pm	Remained in Billets at GENTELLES weather fine Strength 30 officers 1005 other Ranks	
GENTELLES	10/10/15	6pm	Remained in Billets at GENTELLES weather fine Strength 30 officers 1002 other Ranks 3 men transferred to England Sick	
GENTELLES	11/10/15	6pm	Remained in Billets at GENTELLES weather fine Strength 30 officers 1002 other Ranks	
GENTELLES	12/10/15	6pm	Remained in Billets at GENTELLES weather fine Strength 30 officers 1001 other Ranks one man transferred to ENGLAND Sick	
GENTELLES	13/10/15	6pm	Remained in Billets at GENTELLES weather fine Strength 30 officers 1001 other Ranks Received orders to proceed to VILLERS BRETONNEAUX on 14th	
VILLERS BRETONNEAUX	14/10/15	6pm	Marched off from GENTELLES at 9.45 am and arrived at our Billets at VILLERS BRETONNEAUX at 11.15 am weather misty Strength 30 officers 1001 other ranks Received orders to move off at 6.50am the next morning	

Army Form C. 2118.

WAR DIARY
or
INTELLIGENCE SUMMARY.
(Erase heading not required.)

Place	Date	Hour	Summary of Events and Information	Remarks and references to Appendices
VILLERS BOCAGE	15/6/15	8 pm	Marched off at 6.50 am via CORBIE, PONT NOYELLS, QUERRIEUX to VILLERS BOCAGE, and carried out a forced reconnaissance on the way being inspected by General Watson 12th Corps Commander. Arrived at VILLERS BOCAGE about 4 pm and billeted for the night. Weather fine. Strength 29 officers 928 men 1 officer and 43 other ranks being left at VILLERS BRETONNEUX.	JJ
VILLERS BRETONNEAUX	16/6/15	6pm	Marched off from VILLERS BOCAGE at 8.50 am Road via RAINNEVILLE, QUERRIEUX, PONT NOYELLS, CORBIE to VILLERS BRETONNEAUX arriving about 1.30 pm. Inspected by General when 12th Corps Commander at CORBIE about 12.15 pm. Weather fine. Strength 30 officers 1050 other ranks. 1 man transferred to ENGLAND Sick.	JJ
VILLERS BRETONNEAUX	17/6/15	6pm	Remained in Billets at VILLERS BRETONNEAUX. Weather fine. Strength 30 officers 1000 other ranks.	JJ

Army Form C. 2118.

WAR DIARY
or
INTELLIGENCE SUMMARY.
(Erase heading not required.)

Instructions regarding War Diaries and Intelligence Summaries are contained in F. S. Regs., Part II. and the Staff Manual respectively. Title pages will be prepared in manuscript.

Place	Date	Hour	Summary of Events and Information	Remarks and references to Appendices
VILLERS BRETONNEAUX	18/10/15	6pm	Remained in Billets at VILLERS BRETONNEAUX weather fine Strength 30 Officers 1000 other ranks.	L/F
VILLERS BRETONNEAUX	19/10/15	6pm	Remained in Billets at VILLERS BRETONNEAUX weather fine Strength 30 Officers 1000 other Ranks	L/F
VILLERS BRETONNEAUX	20/10/15	6 A.M.	Remained in Billets at VILLERS BRETONNEAUX weather fine Strength 30 Officers 1000 other Ranks	L/F
VILLER BOCAGE	21/10/15	6 P.m	Marched out of VILLERS BRETONNEAUX at 10.10 a.m. and arrived at VILLER BOCAGE at 5.30pm and went into billets Strength 30 Officers and 1000 other ranks. weather fine.	L/F
VILLER BOCAGE	22/10/15	6pm	Remained in Billets at VILLER BOCAGE weather fine Strength 30 Officers 1000 other ranks	L/F
VILLER BOCAGE	23/10/15	6pm	Remained in Billets at VILLER BOCAGE weather fine but cold. Strength 30 Officers 1000 other ranks.	L/F

Army Form C. 2118.

WAR DIARY
or
INTELLIGENCE SUMMARY.

(Erase heading not required.)

Instructions regarding War Diaries and Intelligence Summaries are contained in F. S. Regs., Part II. and the Staff Manual respectively. Title pages will be prepared in manuscript.

Place	Date	Hour	Summary of Events and Information	Remarks and references to Appendices
VILLER BOCAGE	24/10/15	6pm	Remained in VILLER BOCAGE weather cold & wet Strength 30 Officers & 1000 other Ranks.	
VILLER BOCAGE	25/10/15	6pm	Remained in VILLER BOCAGE weather cold & wet Strength 30 Officers & 1000 other Ranks.	
VILLER BOCAGE	26/10/15	6pm	Remained in VILLER BOCAGE weather fine Strength 30 Officers & 1000 other Ranks.	
FRECHENCOURT	27/10/15	6pm	Marched out of VILLER BOCAGE at 10am via RAINNEVILLE to FRECHENCOURT and billeted for the night month out L.H. and Strength 30 Officers & 1000 other ranks	
MEAULTE	28/10/15	6pm	Marched out of FRECHENCOURT via FRANVILLERS, HEILLY BUIRE DERANCOURT and billeted 3cys at MEAULTE one coy at BECORDEL. Attached 54th Brigade 18Div for instruction in trenches weather wet Strength 30 Officers 1000 other ranks.	

Army Form C. 2118.

WAR DIARY
or
INTELLIGENCE SUMMARY.
(Erase heading not required.)

Place	Date	Hour	Summary of Events and Information	Remarks and references to Appendices
MEAULTE	29/6/15	6pm	Remained in Billets at MEAULTE. 2 The officers & 2 Co's under instruction in the trenches with 7D Bedfords & 6th Northants for 24 hours. Weather fine. Strength 30 officers 1000 other ranks.	ff
MEAULTE	30/6/15	6pm	Remained in Billets at MEAULTE. Remaining 2 of officers & 2 Co's under instruction in the trenches. Weather wet. Strength 30 officers 1000 other ranks.	ff
LA NEUVILLE	31/6/15	6pm	Received orders at 11am to move to LA NEUVILLE. Marched off at 2pm via BUIRE & BONNAY arriving at 5.30pm. Weather wet. Strength 30 officers & 1000 others.	ff

Lt Col C.L.H Spencer Lieut Colonel
7 Wilts Regiment

www.ingramcontent.com/pod-product-compliance
Lightning Source LLC
Chambersburg PA
CBHW081247170426
43191CB00037B/2064